GOD FAMILY WORK

GFW

DESIGNED IN USA

AUTHORS: MATTHEW BIALLO · AUBRY BIALLO · JAMES TUNSTALL · URSULA TUNSTALL

• • • This • • •

DEVOTIONAL

BELONGS TO:

IF FOUND PLEASE RETURN TO

INDEX

INTRODUCTION

FOR A GODLY HUSBAND

MARRIAGE DEVOTIONAL

Marriage is a profound partnership, deeply rooted in the earliest stories of creation. Just as Eve stood beside Adam as his companion and helper, every wife is called to support and stand with her husband. But remember, this call for unity and support is not about one being above the other. Both partners, equal in God's eyes, come together in harmony as they fulfill their roles outlined in scripture.

This devotional aims to guide couples in nurturing a God-centered home. It is here, in the heart of the family, that faith takes root, grows, and blossoms. We will explore the importance of oneness, dive deeper into scripture on taboo topics, and get past any awkwardness. We'll discover God's love and divine purpose for your family.

But beyond roles and responsibilities, at the heart of this journey lies the relationship with God and our spouse. As we venture through these pages, you'll be challenged to dig deep, grow vulnerable, and build trust. With God at the center, everything aligns beautifully. Embark on this devotional adventure to embrace your calling in marriage. By doing so, we hope you'll draw closer to God and weave a stronger bond with your spouse.

Let's begin this journey together.

Dear God, we invite You into this journey to guide the reader and bless them in their reading, devotion, and thoughts. I pray that they will be open to hearing Your voice and that Your Holy Spirit will guide them through their journey in this devotional. May Your Wisdom begin to penetrate their heart even now, and that you birth an excitement in them for seeking Your ways for their relationship with their spouse. Thank You God for bringing this book into the hands of this reader, and I pray that You would encounter them with Your manifest presence while they seek a marriage rooted in You. Amen

THIS BOOKS INTENDED USE

This devotional is designed for couples. Whether you're just starting your marital journey or reigniting its spark, this book offers guidance and hands on practices. With 50 enriching lessons, drawing from the biblical perspective of marriage, it celebrates the union of both a man and a woman as intended by God. But remember, it's not a race! Feel free to move through the lessons at a pace that feels right for you and your spouse. We hope this book offers insight, healing, and strengthens your bond, guiding you closer to God's plan for your relationship.

You can expect a consistent layout throughout each category that will help guide you through each topic. Here's what it will look like.

1. Topics: Each category is broken down into topics. Take your time to understand each one before moving forward.

2. Scripture References: Be rooted in God's Word. These verses will offer clarity that you can reference for deeper personal study.

3. Challenges: Thought-provoking ideas and actions tailored for each topic. We pray these challenges strengthen your bond with God and your spouse.

4. Reply Area: A space to jot down your thoughts, experiences, or any `aha!' moments during challenges.

Challenge

Read the list of categories we cover in this book. Next to each category subject, write down a word or phrase describing how you feel about each. Once you're done, take a moment to review this list with your spouse, taking turns discussing your feelings for each category.

Challenge Reply

Roles in Marriage ______________________________

God Comes First ______________________________

Your First Priority ______________________________

Friends, Lovers, Partners ______________________________

Basics of Communication ______________________________

Gift of Prayer ______________________________

Dealing with Conflict ______________________________

Relationship and Family ______________________________

Soul Ties ______________________________

Sex in Marriage ______________________________

Overcoming Lust Issues ______________________________

All About Money ______________________________

Fruitful and Responsible ______________________________

Focusing Our Time ______________________________

Covering the Family ______________________________

ROLES
in
MARRIAGE

A HUSBANDS ROLE

As a husband, you are the head of your household, meaning you have a great responsibility for the decisions made within your home. However, this does not mean that you should act as a dictator. Instead, you are called to love your wife as Christ loves the church. This means that you should include her in the decision-making process for your home as much as possible. After all, if you love your wife, you would want to hear her opinion on important matters.

It is important to remember that, ultimately, God will hold you accountable for the decisions made in your home. As the head of your household, you are called to lead your family physically and spiritually. This means that when making decisions, you should consider how they will impact your family in practical terms and how they will impact your family's spiritual growth. If you are faced with a decision that will benefit your home but negatively affect your spiritual life, you should carefully consider whether it is the right choice.

Your wife is the head of your children, and you are the head of your wife. In my own marriage, I allow my wife to make most of the decisions regarding our children and their upbringing, as she is the one who primarily cares for them. However, as the head of the home, it is still your responsibility to ensure that all decisions made in your home are pleasing to the Lord.

As the head of your home, you are also called to pastor your family. This means that you are responsible for the spiritual growth of your wife and children. While the church can provide support and guidance, it is ultimately your job to ensure that your family is learning biblical principles and growing closer to God. This means you should prioritize prayer, fasting, and reading the Bible as a family.

Finally, it is essential to remember that as the head of your household, you are also called to be a provider. While the world may equate being a provider with long hours at work, it is important to remember that providing for your family means more than just financial support. You should carefully consider which job will best suit your family's financial and practical needs. For example, is it more important to have a brand new car or more time to spend with your loved ones?

"THE WOMAN WAS MADE OF A RIB OUT OF THE SIDE OF ADAM; NOT MADE OUT OF HIS HEAD TO RULE OVER HIM, NOR OUT OF HIS FEET TO BE TRAMPLED UPON BY HIM, BUT OUT OF HIS SIDE TO BE EQUAL WITH HIM, UNDER HIS ARM TO BE PROTECTED, AND NEAR HIS HEART TO BE BELOVED."

From the Bible commentary of Matthew Henry

Scripture References

Husbands as Head, but not as Dictators
Ephesians 5:23 + Colossians 3:19

Loving Your Wife as Christ Loves the Church
Ephesians 5:25

Accountability Before God
Hebrews 13:17

Wife's Role in the Family and Mutual Submission
Proverbs 31:27-28 + Ephesians 5:21

Leading the Family Spiritually
Deuteronomy 6:6-7 + Joshua 24:15

The Role of a Provider
1 Timothy 5:8 + Proverbs 22:1

Challenge

What areas do you need to work on most? Are you leading a godly home? Do you love your wife and guide her spiritually? Take some time to think about some ways you can take this teaching and apply it to your life in the role you have as a husband. Write down your goals and plans moving forward in this role so you can refer back to them later.

GOD

COMES

First

LEADING A GODLY HOME

As the head of the home, it is your responsibility to ensure the physical and spiritual well-being of your household. Once you are married, it is crucial to understand that you are moving away from your parents and starting your own family. You are responsible for your own family now, and you must make sure that the order of priorities in your home aligns with God's will.

As a Christian, your foremost priority should be to seek God and put Him first. This means putting God before your spouse, children, and all other relationships. When you make God your top priority, all other aspects of your life will fall into place. It is important to actively pursue God, allowing Him to transform you into the man of God He has called you to be.

This transformation will make you a stronger and more effective leader for your home, spouse, and children. By putting God first, you can fulfill your role as a husband and follow God's will for marriage.

As a husband, leading a godly home should be a top priority. By putting God first and pursuing Him wholeheartedly, you can become the leader that your family needs and fulfill God's plan for your marriage. Remember, your ultimate goal as a husband is to bring glory to God. You will fulfill this purpose by prioritizing your relationship with Him and focusing on leading a godly home. Trust in God to guide you as you seek to honor Him in all areas of your life.

Scripture References

Prioritize and Align Home Life with God's Will
Genesis 2:24

Role of a Husband in Marriage
Ephesians 5:25-28

Leading a Godly Home
Proverbs 22:6

Challenge

What is one way you can actively pursue God? Make an effort to implement this into your life going forward. Write down your plan below to reference later.

YOUR *First* PRIORITY

JOINED TO YOUR WIFE

The Bible tells us that a man leaves his father and mother and is joined to his wife, and the two become one. I have seen today how husbands will go back to their parents for support when there is conflict in their marriage instead of talking it out with their wives. This chapter is neither about conflict nor family issues, but we will get to it later. However, it is essential to note that you have been joined to your wife and have become one. Your wife now becomes your top priority and responsibility. We already know God comes first in all things, but after God comes your wife.

We are instructed to love our wives as our own bodies. After all, this is the person God has given us to spend the rest of our lives with. The love we are instructed to have for our wives is the same love God has for the church. It's a sacrificial love. Are you willing to sacrifice things that are important to you for your wife? Getting married is no small thing; you are now half of a whole. According to God, we are supposed to do everything we can to serve the other half as best as possible.

To be united means to walk together in agreement, support and encourage each other, and work as a team to pursue God's purposes for your lives. It involves open communication, active listening, and resolving conflicts with love and respect. Unity requires sacrifice, humility, and a willingness to lay aside individual preferences for the sake of the marriage.

As husbands, we are not called to be masters over our wives but to serve them in humility and love. Take the time to learn what your wife needs and how you can better serve her. Doing so will reduce her worries, troubles, and pressures and create a strong, loving bond between the two of you. Remember that your wife is a gift from God, and it is our responsibility as husbands to honor that gift by serving and loving her as Christ loves us.

Scripture References

Leaving and Cleaving
Genesis 2:24

Loving Wives as Our Own Bodies
Ephesians 5:28-29

Sacrificial Love
Ephesians 5:25

Unity in Marriage
Amos 3:3

Serving in Humility
Mark 10:43-45

Honoring the Wife as a Gift from God
Proverbs 18:22

Challenge

Ask your wife one way you can better serve her. Record her answer below. Take some time to study her response. Write down how you are going to implement this.

____

____

____

____

____

____

____

____

Friends

LOVERS

PARTNERS

INTAMACY NOT SEX

In the divine institution of marriage, God has ordained that two individuals become one, a unity that is more than just physical. While sexual intimacy can be a profound and beautiful expression of love, it alone does not fully embody the depth of our affection for one another. In contemporary society, many women feel compelled to offer sex to demonstrate love. At the same time, men often demand it as proof of love. However, true love is revealed through intimacy, which surpasses the physical act of sex.

Men and women often have different understandings of intimacy. I have often heard women say intimacy starts first thing in the morning. It is the little things men do throughout the day for women. For men, it is often about physical contact. You can see how God created us differently. That is why it is essential to understand and work at a marriage and be intimate with your spouse.

Intimacy entails sharing the innermost parts of ourselves with our spouse, allowing them to behold the depths of our being. It is a mutual vulnerability that invites our partner to see into us, forging a closeness that intertwines our lives and entwines our hearts and souls. God, in His wisdom, designed this for a purpose: through intimacy, we can genuinely attain oneness with our beloved.

To be intimate with your partner, you need to trust them. It means you must become vulnerable and take the risk of opening your heart up to them. It doesn't have to happen all at once. The journey can take time while you grow together and trust one another. Be honest with yourself so you can be real with your spouse and accept and encourage one another. Together, you can build each other up and lift each other up before God.

Scripture References

Oneness in Marriage
Genesis 2:24

Expressions of Love Beyond Physicality
1 Corinthians 13:4-7

Differences in Intimacy Perceptions
1 Peter 3:7

Intimacy and Vulnerability
James 5:16

Growing Together in Trust
Ecclesiastes 4:9-10

Challenge

Take a moment to think of something that makes you vulnerable. Something you have never shared with your spouse. Write it down below and then take a moment to share it with your spouse. Remember to be understanding with whatever they choose to share with you.

DATING YOUR SPOUSE

Courting shouldn't end when you get married. We must be intentional about our growth as a couple and continue to focus on each other through the seasons of life. There will be moments in marriage when it gets difficult to focus on each other. For example, with children, finding a moment alone with your spouse may become difficult, but you must devise a plan.

You and your spouse need time alone to be intimate, to laugh, and to date. Date nights are a vital part of any marriage. Making this small commitment will create a time when you can focus on one another without any distractions. An intentional time together will strengthen your relationship while keeping your priorities first.

Make it romantic and fun; remember when you first started dating and how much effort you put into seeing each other. Do you remember the sacrifices you made to make your spouse happy? This urge should not die with marriage or time. Keep the fire going. God's word calls you to love each other, and this is an area where you can make an effort to really show your love.

Remove the distractions during these special moments with your spouse. Turn off the devices, put them away, and focus on building that relationship with your spouse. Forget the chores and responsibilities for a few hours while you focus all your energy and love on one another. Date nights can look different depending on the couple, but it should never be a thing of the past. Take time to be intentional and face-to-face with your spouse and sacrifice to make date night special for your spouse.

May you heed the biblical call to honor and nurture your marital relationship as you embark on these intentional moments together. By fostering these moments, you cultivate a bond that blossoms with love, joy, and shared experiences. Don't let the flame of your romance burn out.

Scripture References

Intentional Time Together
Ecclesiastes 4:9-10

Recapturing Early Romance
Revelation 2:4-5

Loving Actively and Intentionally
1 Corinthians 13:4-7

Removing Distractions
Hebrews 12:1-2

The Sanctity of Marriage
Hebrews 13:4

Challenge

Take some time to plan some dates with your spouse. Is it something you can schedule on a continuous basis? Write down your plan below and be intentional about committing to it.

LOVE US LIKE

It is not enough to fulfill our marital duties or carry out the responsibilities expected of a spouse. Our love should extend beyond mere obligation. We are called to genuinely like and enjoy our spouse, valuing their presence and cherishing their companionship.

Sometimes, during marriage, we may find ourselves in a situation where we love our spouse but struggle to genuinely like them. This can manifest in various ways, such as feeling disconnected or disinterested in spending time together or lacking an eagerness to listen and understand one another.

It is essential to address this in order to cultivate a healthy and God-honoring marriage. We should actively seek to nurture not only love but also a deep liking for our spouse. This involves investing time and effort into building a genuine friendship and companionship. Engaging in shared activities, pursuing common interests, and prioritizing quality time together can foster a stronger liking and emotional connection.

While it is important to appreciate our spouse's role in providing for our needs and fulfilling their responsibilities, we must be cautious not to fall into the trap of loving an idealized version of a spouse set by the world. True marital fulfillment comes from both loving and liking our spouse in their entirety, with their strengths, weaknesses, and unique qualities.

Our spouse should not only be our life partner but also our best friend. Through the ups and downs, the joys and sorrows, we are called to walk hand in hand, supporting and cherishing one another. Together, we navigate life's journey and embracing our vows: of for better or for worse, for richer or for poorer, in sickness and health.

May we not only love our spouse sacrificially but also genuinely like them, celebrating their presence, enjoying their company, and building a deep and lasting friendship. In doing so, we honor the divine design for marriage and experience the blessings of a truly fulfilling and joyous union.

Scripture References

The Foundation of Marriage Vows
Ecclesiastes 4:9-12

Love Beyond Obligation
1 Corinthians 13:1-3

Valuing Companionship
Song of Solomon 5:16

Building Friendship in Marriage
Proverbs 17:17

Seeing Beyond the Surface
1 Samuel 16:7

Challenge

Make a list of 5 things you like about your spouse and take turns reading them to each other.

HOW TO LOVE HER

Loving your wife is not just a mere obligation, but a beautiful privilege and sacred calling God has entrusted you. As a husband, you are called to love your wife in a way that reflects the love of Christ for His Church.

First and foremost, love your wife unconditionally, just as Christ loves the church. Show her sacrificial love, putting her needs and well-being above your own. The Bible tells us in Ephesians 5:25 "Husbands, love your wives, just as Christ loved the church and gave himself up for her." Your love should be selfless and unwavering.

Communicate with your wife openly and honestly. Take the time to truly listen to her thoughts, feelings, and desires. Proverbs 18:13 reminds us to answer before listening–that is folly and shame. Seek to understand her and her emotions. Create an environment where she feels safe to express herself.

Cherish and honor your wife. Treat her with respect, dignity, and kindness. Show her gratitude for all that she does for you and your family. Proverbs 31:28 states, Her children rise up and call her blessed; her husband also, and he praises her. Let your words and actions affirm her worth and value. I heard a saying once that I love If you always treat your wife like a queen, you will always be king∫.

Lead your family with wisdom and humility. As the head of the household, it is your responsibility to lead with integrity and seek God's guidance. Ephesians 5:23 reminds us, For the husband is the head of the wife as Christ is the head of the church, his body, of which he is the Savior. Lead by example, demonstrating godly character and making decisions that honor God and your family.

Support and encourage your wife's dreams and aspirations. Be her biggest fan, encouraging her to pursue her passions and gifts. Help her grow spiritually, emotionally, and intellectually. Proverbs 31:29-30 says Many women do noble things, but you surpass them all. Charm is deceptive, and beauty is fleeting, but a woman who fears the Lord is to be praised.

Finally, love your wife faithfully and commit to your marriage covenant. Remain loyal and faithful, honoring your vows before God and man. Seek to cultivate a deep emotional and physical intimacy with your wife. Proverbs 5:18-19 reminds us "May your fountain be blessed, and may you rejoice in the wife of your youth. A loving doe, a graceful deer–may her breasts satisfy you always, may you ever be intoxicated with her love."

In summary, loving your wife is a divine calling. It involves sacrificial love, open communication, honor, leadership, support, and faithfulness. By following these biblical principles, you will create a strong and loving foundation for your marriage, reflecting the love of Christ.

Scripture References

Loving your Wife Reflects Christ's Love for the Church
Ephesians 5:25

Open Communication is Vital
Proverbs 18:13

Honor and Value your Wife
Proverbs 31:28

The Role of Leadership in Marriage
Ephesians 5:23

Commitment and Faithfulness
Proverbs 5:18-19

Challenge

Think about some ways you can put her needs above your own. Write them down below and then be intentional about implementing them.

HER LOVE LANGUAGE

Understanding and speaking your husband's love language is essential to nurturing a deep and intimate connection with him. Just as you desire to be loved in a way that resonates with your heart, your husband also has unique needs and desires that are important to consider. By discovering and embracing his love language, you can communicate your love in a way that truly speaks to his soul.

The Bible reminds us of the significance of love and its transformative power in relationships. Love is patient, kind, and selfless. It seeks to understand, support, and encourage. As a wife, you have the incredible opportunity to embody these qualities as you seek to love your husband in a way that aligns with his love language.

The concept of love languages, as described by Gary Chapman, suggests that individuals have different ways of giving and receiving love. These love languages are acts of service, words of affirmation, quality time, physical touch, and receiving gifts. Discovering your husband's primary love language can significantly enhance your ability to express your love and meet his deepest emotional needs.

If your husband's love language is acts of service, you can show your love by serving him in practical ways. Whether cooking his favorite meal or going out of your way to do something special for him, your acts of service communicate care and devotion.

If his love language is words of affirmation, use the power of your words to uplift and encourage him. Express your admiration, appreciation, and respect. Offer words of praise and affirm his character, accomplishments, and efforts. Your affirming words can strengthen his spirit and nurture his confidence.

For a husband whose love language is quality time, intentionally spend uninterrupted and focused time together. Engage in activities that he enjoys, have meaningful conversations, and create lasting memories. By giving him your undivided attention, you communicate that he is a priority in your life.

If physical touch is your husband's primary love language, express your love through affectionate gestures. Hold his hand, give hugs, offer gentle caresses, and be responsive to his need for physical closeness. Physical touch can deepen emotional connection and provide a sense of security and belonging.

Lastly, if receiving gifts is your husband's love language, thoughtful and meaningful gifts can speak volumes of your love and care. It's not about the monetary value but the thought and effort behind the gift. Surprise him with small gestures of love and appreciation, showing you have him in mind.

Remember, understanding your husband's love language is just the beginning. True love requires ongoing effort, patience, and a genuine desire to meet each other's needs. Seek God's wisdom and guidance as you navigate the intricacies of your marriage, and let His love be the foundation of your relationship.

May your journey of discovering and speaking your husband's love language bring you closer together, strengthen your bond, and reflect the love of Christ in your marriage.

Challenge

Take the love language test by searching for The 5 Love Languages test online, share your results with your spouse.

HOW WOMEN ARE WIRED

As you seek to understand and support your wife, it is essential to recognize and appreciate how she is uniquely wired. God has created women with distinct desires, emotions, and needs in His wisdom. Understanding and honoring these aspects of your wife's identity can foster a deeper and more fulfilling intimate connection in your marriage.

First and foremost, it is crucial to approach your wife's sexuality with love, respect, and selflessness. The Bible reminds us in Ephesians 5:25 "Husbands, love your wives, just as Christ loved the church and gave himself up for her." Your love for your wife should mirror Christ's sacrificial love, placing her needs and desires above your own.

One crucial aspect of your wife's sexual and intimate nature is the significance of emotional connection. For many women, a strong emotional bond serves as a foundation for their sexual desire and fulfillment. Taking the time to understand your wife's emotional needs, engaging in meaningful conversations, and cultivating intimacy outside of the bedroom can significantly enhance your sexual relationship.

Communication is vital in fostering a healthy and satisfying sexual connection with your wife. Each woman may have different preferences, desires, and boundaries regarding intimacy. It is essential to have open and honest conversations with your wife, expressing your desires while listening attentively to hers. Seek to create a safe space where she feels comfortable sharing her thoughts, needs, and concerns.

Additionally, it is essential to recognize that your wife's sexual response may differ from yours. While men often experience more immediate physical arousal, women may require more time, emotional connection, and foreplay to fully engage in sexual intimacy. Patience, understanding, and attentiveness to your wife's unique needs can contribute to a more enjoyable and fulfilling sexual experience for both of you.

Moreover, it is crucial to approach your sexual relationship with a servant's heart. The Bible teaches us to honor and cherish our spouses. 1 Corinthians 7:3-4 states, The husband should fulfill his marital duty to his wife, and likewise the wife to her husband. The wife does not have authority over her own body but yields it to her husband. In the same way, the husband does not have authority over his own body but yields it to his wife. Your sexual relationship should be marked by mutual love, care, and selflessness as you seek to meet each other's needs and desires.

Lastly, remember that your wife's sexual and intimate nature is a gift from God. It is a sacred and beautiful aspect of your marriage covenant. By approaching it with reverence, understanding, and a desire to honor God's design, you can nurture a deep and intimate connection that reflects the love and unity found in Christ and His church.

May you seek God's wisdom, guidance, and strength as you navigate the intricate and beautiful journey of sexual and intimate connection with your wife. May your love for her reflect the selfless love of Christ, bringing joy, fulfillment, and spiritual growth to your marriage.

Scripture References

Biblical Foundations for Loving Your Wife
Ephesians 5:25

Approach to Sexual Relationship in Marriage
1 Corinthians 7:3-4

Challenge

Write a list of your turn-ons and turn-offs. Take turns discussing them with your spouse.

BASICS *of* COMMUNICATION

LISTEN TO HER

Ask anyone what the main problem is after their conflict is resolved, and you will find out that many times, it's a lack of communication. The root issue of many fights between married couples is bad communication. If there is an area of unrest in your relationship with your spouse, have you talked to them about it?

So often, we convince ourselves that the issue will take care of itself and that it's unimportant or maybe even too small to address. These same issues can be used to fuel a disagreement into an argument. Do not harbor anything from your spouse; use communication to your advantage. Always talk with your spouse about how you are feeling and thinking.

Talking about small inconveniences or minor disagreements can easily keep you and your spouse on the same page and even bring you closer together. I love knowing what my spouse is thinking, and it makes me feel closer to her when we are both in unity. This can be achieved just by listening first and then sharing what's on your heart. It's not complicated, but it is easier said than done. As the Bible teaches us in Ephesians 4:29 "Let no corrupting talk come out of your mouths, but only such as is good for building up, as fits the occasion, that it may give grace to those who hear."

The Bible tells us if one gives an answer before he hears, it is foolish. That's why you always want to make sure you listen to what your spouse has to say before you react and respond. Otherwise, you'll only be focused on responding and won't hear what they have to share with you. Be vulnerable with your spouse and learn to trust them with your feelings, and in return, they should do the same. Remember, two are better than one because they have a good reward for their toil. Work together with your spouse to overcome any obstacles, and your marriage will be stronger for it.

Scripture References

Biblical Guidance on Communication
Ephesians 4:29

Listening Before Reacting
Proverbs 18:13

The Power of Unity in Marriage
Ecclesiastes 4:9

Challenge

Write down one of your recent disagreements with your spouse. Take time discussing both your points of view and LISTENING to her points. See if you can find out what caused the issue.

GIFT

of

PRAYER

GOD'S INTIMACY

God, who knew you even before you were born, desires an intimate relationship with you. You do not need to hide anything from Him because He already knows everything about you, even the parts you keep hidden from others. While people judge you based on your current circumstances, God sees you through the lens of your potential, knowing what He has ordained you to become.

God looks at us differently than how man looks at us. He sees our potential. He is the Alpha and Omega, the beginning and the end. God is omniscient and sees all things. When everyone else judges us by our current circumstances, God sees us in the future and knows the plans He has for us.

I say all that to encourage you to seek God intimately. When you seek Him in prayer, seek Him with your whole heart; seek Him with everything you have. Do this because He takes pleasure in it. He loves you, and He loves for you to share everything you have with Him. God is calling us to go deeper with Him, and that starts with you surrendering that masked appearance the world has taught you to hide behind. If this is something that you struggle with, be honest with God and surrender it to Him.

Scripture References

God's Intimate Knowledge and Relationship
Jeremiah 1:5 + Psalm 139:1-2

God's Perspective vs. Man's Perspective
Jeremiah 29:11 + Revelation 1:8 + Psalm 147:5

The Call to Deepen Our Relationship with God
Jeremiah 29:13 + Psalm 37:4 + Psalm 55:22

Challenge

Write down below some ways you see yourself. When you are done take a moment to pray and ask God how He sees you. Write down what you think He is saying to you.

SEEKING GOD FIRST

We will face stress, worry, fear, and doubt in life. No matter how hopeless your situation may feel, the Bible assures us that we can overcome it through faith in God. In Matthew 6:31-33 "Jesus tells us not to worry about our basic needs but instead to seek God's kingdom and His righteousness, and all these things will be provided for us."

God wants us to seek Him in times of turbulence. He instructs us to turn to Him and seek His face. We should take our troubles straight to God when they happen and seek His comfort and guidance. God is already waiting for you when things go wrong. He is waiting with open arms, ready to comfort you. He is enough, and He alone can completely cover and deliver you from anything and everything that would come against you.

He promises to be our refuge and our strength, an ever-present help in trouble. When you're going through struggles in your marriage, seek God First. He is the one who created your spouse and knows them even better than you. We can trust in Him and lean on Him for support and guidance. Instead of turning to worldly comforts, we should turn to God and pray, read His Word, and worship Him. This is the way to receive the peace that passes understanding. God is faithful and true, and He will never leave us or forsake us.

Scripture References

Overcoming Stress, Worry, Fear, and Doubt Through Faith
Matthew 6:31-33

Seeking God in Turbulent Times
Psalm 28:7 + Isaiah 66:13

God as Our Refuge and Strength
Psalm 46:1

The Call to Turn to God
Philippians 4:6-7 + Hebrews 13:5

Challenge

Write some things you are struggling with below. Then, take a moment to pray to God about each of them, taking special care to hand them over to Him and His will for each situation.

DEALING • • • *with* • • • CONFLICT

GROWING IN FORGIVENESS

Forgiveness is a fundamental teaching in the Bible and essential to our relationship with God and others. Forgiveness is not always easy, but it is necessary. Holding onto unforgiveness gives the enemy a foothold in our lives, and it can fester and grow, leading to destruction.

The devil loves it when we hold onto unforgiveness. It gives him a stronghold in our lives and a foothold in our hearts. This is the plan of the enemy for you. If that unforgiveness continues to fester and grow, becoming deeply rooted, he can use it to hold you or others back.

The Bible tells us that our fight is not against flesh and blood but against the rulers, against the authorities, against the powers of this dark world, and against the spiritual forces of evil in the heavenly realms. This scripture encourages us to forgive others because it shows us that our fight is not against man. The Bible also instructs us to forgive others in order for us to be forgiven. Chances are you have hurt someone and may be the reason for someone else's unforgiveness. The same enemy that attacks you to hold onto unforgiveness can attack others to harbor offense in their heart for you.

God has given us the authority to forgive our brothers and sisters and to be forgiven and covered by the blood of Jesus. This was no small sacrifice for Jesus. You are not responsible for harboring any offense as a son or daughter of God. Give it to Him, and release any pain, evil thoughts, or ill will for others. You will feel lighter, stronger, and closer to God when you do.

Forgiveness is not a one-time event. Checking yourself for unforgiveness is an ongoing issue we will have to deal with all our lives because people will hurt you and let you down. It requires us to search our hearts and continually release our hurts and pains to God. When we do this, we experience the peace that surpasses all understanding and the joy that comes from being in right relationship with God and others. So, if you are struggling with unforgiveness, give it to God today. Let Him take your pain and hurt and replace it with His love and grace.

Scripture References

The Importance of Forgiveness
Matthew 6:14-15

Unforgiveness as a Foothold for the Enemy
Ephesians 4:26-27

Our Battle is Spiritual
Ephesians 6:12

Releasing Offense to God
Psalm 55:22:

God's Forgiveness through Jesus
Colossians 1:13-14

Challenge

Write down a list of people you need to forgive, or anyone you hold any type of grudge towards. If you're not sure, its okay to add them just in case. When your list is complete take some time to pray about each person, asking God to help you forgive and release them.

CONFLICT & DISCRETION

In marriage, conflict is inevitable, but it is essential to handle it in a way that honors God and your spouse. The Bible teaches us to be one with our spouse and support them, so it is essential to keep conflict between the two of you. Seeking guidance from wise friends or a parent can be helpful. Still, avoiding putting your spouse down or influencing the other person's opinion is vital. Instead, seek counsel with an open mind and a neutral attitude so you can hear what the other person has to say.

It is also important to keep the conflict private and not make your spouse look like "the bad person" to others just because he disagrees with you. This does not mean you should hide your conflicts or pretend everything is perfect, but rather keep them between you and your spouse. Remember, the enemy loves to create division and chaos in our relationships, so staying united with your spouse is essential.

When conflicts are difficult to resolve, seek counsel from God first. If necessary, you can ask for help from trusted individuals who will provide godly advice without taking sides or interfering with your relationship. Let your marriage be a testament to God's love and grace, even amid conflicts.

Scripture References

Unity in Marriage
Genesis 2:24

The Importance of Taming the Tongue and Avoiding Gossip
Proverbs 21:23 + Proverbs 16:28

The Enemy's Intent to Create Division
1 Peter 5:8

Seeking Godly Counsel
Proverbs 15:22

Peacemaking and Resolution
Matthew 5:9

Challenge

Write down some ways you have neglected keeping your conflicts with your spouse private. Include any ways you have put your spouse down while seeking council. Study these to make sure going forward you keep the integrity of your spouse, making sure you honor them even when disagreements arise.

FIGHTING IT OUT

How often during a fight have you been so set on your point of view that you are constantly on the defensive? You are so focused on responding to what someone else has already said that you aren't even listening to what they are saying. It's easy to stay arrogant, prideful, and angry when arguing, but did you know the Bible instructs us to neither be angry nor prideful?

When there is fighting, rather than letting your insecurities guide the conversation, listen to what the Bible has to say about conflict. Remember, the devil wants you to fight face to face because he knows how dangerous you are fighting shoulder to shoulder. The Bible tells us to be quick to listen, slow to speak, and slow to become angry.

Speak with love when there is conflict. Do nothing out of selfish ambition or vain conceit. You are instructed to value others above yourself, prioritizing the needs and interests of others over your own. There is a calm way to approach conflict in your marriage. Listen to what your spouse has to say, focus on why it is important to them, and then communicate with them about why you may have a different point of view. Only by looking at the situation from all points of view will you come to a conclusion together.

To resolve conflict, listening to your spouse and understanding their perspective is important. Communicate with them about your point of view, and work together to find a solution that works for both of you. Marriage is a battle but not a battle against each other. As a team, you are called to fight against the enemy's attacks and gain ground for the Kingdom of God. So, approach conflict with prayer, love, humility, and a willingness to work together towards a common goal.

Scripture References

The Dangers of Anger, Arrogance, and Pride
Ephesians 4:26 + Proverbs 16:18

Guidance on Handling Conflict
James 1:19 + Philippians 2:3

Approaching Conflict with Love
Proverbs 18:2 + Matthew 5:9

Unity in Marriage and Fighting Together
Genesis 2:24 + Ephesians 6:12

Challenge

Think about a disagreement you have had with your spouse where you were wrong. Write down what happened and where you went wrong. Identify what the cause of the issue was (for example not listening or being prideful).

GOSSIP

and

COMPLAINING

"BALL & CHAIN"

As a husband, it is crucial to always treat your spouse with respect. Engaging in conversations where you belittle, complain about, or gossip about your spouse is unacceptable, especially in the presence of friends. The Bible urges us to live differently from the world around us. Refrain from participating in such conversations, for they do not build up or encourage anyone, especially not your spouse. If there are challenges or issues in your marriage, addressing them together as a team is better.

God's Word explicitly instructs us to handle any problems we may have with our spouse directly. Husbands are called to love their wives, while wives are called to respect their husbands. There is no room for misinterpretation or compromise in these commands. Complaining or gossiping about your spouse with your friends will only create division and distance between you and your partner. Instead, focus on nurturing a relationship of respect, love, and open communication with your spouse, seeking God's guidance and wisdom to overcome challenges together.

Bitterness and complaints aren't always expressed out loud, but they're felt deeply in the heart. Remember, the feelings you hold in your heart towards your wife play a significant role in how you treat her. Ask God to renew your mind and soften your heart towards your spouse. This way, your actions and words towards your partner will also be more kind and loving!

Scripture References

Respect and Love in Marriage
Ephesians 5:25 + Ephesians 5:33

Avoiding Negative Conversations about your Spouse
Ephesians 4:29 + Romans 12:2

Directly Addressing Issues with your Spouse
Matthew 5:23-24

Nurturing a Relationship with Gods Guidance
1 Peter 4:8 + Psalm 127:1

Challenge

Think about some ways you may be belittling your spouse, either knowingly or unknowingly. Write down each occurrence that comes to mind and how you plan on improving moving forward.

GODLY COUNCIL

In our journey of marriage, there may be times when we seek guidance and counsel from others. We must seek advice with a heart and mindset that avoids complaining and gossiping about our spouse. The Bible provides wisdom and guidance on how our words and attitudes should reflect love, respect, and honor toward our spouse.

Complaining about our spouse can harm the health of our marriage and the guidance we receive. Philippians 2:14 instructs us to "Do everything without grumbling or arguing." Instead of focusing on our spouse's faults or shortcomings, we should approach seeking guidance with a positive and solution-oriented mindset. By highlighting our spouse's strengths and positive aspects, we can create an environment that fosters growth and improvement in our relationship.

Gossiping about our spouse contradicts the biblical principles of love and unity within marriage. Proverbs 16:28 warns "A perverse person stirs up conflict, and a gossip separates close friends." Gossip undermines trust, damages relationships, and hinders the effectiveness of the guidance we seek. Instead, we should guard our tongues and choose to speak words that build up and encourage our spouse.

Ephesians 4:29 reminds us "Do not let any unwholesome talk come out of your mouths, but only what is helpful for building others up according to their needs, that it may benefit those who listen." When seeking guidance, we should strive to speak helpful, uplifting, and encouraging words. By avoiding complaining and gossiping, we create an atmosphere of trust, respect, and unity, which leads to more practical guidance and support. Furthermore, Proverbs 11:13 reminds us of the importance of confidentiality and trust within relationships: "A gossip betrays a confidence, but a trustworthy person keeps a secret. When seeking guidance, it is crucial to choose wise and trustworthy individuals." This allows for an environment of openness and vulnerability, where true guidance and understanding can be received.

Scripture References

Avoiding Complaining and Gossip
Philippians 2:14

Gossip Separates and Damages
Proverbs 16:28 + Ephesians

Importance of Confidentiality and Trust
Proverbs 11:13

Challenge

Think about friends and family who you can trust for advice. Make a list of their names below and share it with your spouse. Is this someone you can both trust? Write down what he thinks next to each person.

WISDOM FROM THE WISE

In our journey of faith, there are times when we face challenges, decisions, and uncertainties that require guidance and wisdom beyond our own understanding. The Bible encourages us to seek counsel from those who are wise, mature, and grounded in God's Word. By seeking godly counsel, we open ourselves to valuable insights, perspectives, and advice that can help us navigate through life's complexities in a manner that honors God and aligns with His will.

God has designed us to be in a community, and part of that community includes seeking guidance and counsel from those who possess wisdom and experience in matters of faith and life. Wise counsel can provide clarity, correction, encouragement, and accountability, helping us make sound decisions and avoid potential pitfalls.

When seeking counsel, it is crucial to seek individuals who fear and reverence the Lord. As Psalm 111:10 affirms "The fear of the Lord is the beginning of wisdom; all who follow his precepts have good understanding." It is important to approach individuals who base their advice on the truth of God's Word and seek His guidance in their own lives. Their counsel will be grounded in God's principles and aligned with His purposes.

Identifying wise and trustworthy advisors is a significant aspect of seeking counsel. Proverbs 13:20 advises "Walk with the wise and become wise, for a companion of fools suffers harm." Careful consideration should be given to those we seek counsel from, ensuring that they demonstrate wisdom, godly character, and a deep understanding of Scripture. Seeking individuals who exhibit humility, integrity, and a track record of faithfully following and obeying God is essential.

Before seeking counsel from others, it is essential to approach God in prayer, seeking His wisdom and guidance. James 1:5 assures us, "If any of you lacks wisdom, you should ask God, who gives generously to all without finding fault, and it will be given to you." Seeking God's direction and discernment before seeking counsel allows Him to direct us to thee right people.

Approaching the seeking of counsel with humility and teachability is crucial. Proverbs 19:20 advises "Listen to advice and accept discipline, and at the end, you will be counted among the wise." Recognizing that we do not possess all the answers and being open to correction and guidance is essential. Embracing a teachable spirit that values the wisdom and insights of others allows us to grow in knowledge and understanding.

When receiving counsel, it is important to compare it with the truth of God's Word. Acts 17:11 describes the Berean believers as more noble-minded because they received the message with great eagerness and examined the Scriptures every day to see if what Paul said was true. Testing counsel against the truth of God's Word ensures that it does not contradict or compromise biblical principles. Scripture should be the final authority in determining the validity and alignment of the advice received.

As we receive counsel, it is crucial to seek the guidance of the Holy Spirit to discern how to apply the wisdom received. Proverbs 2:6 reminds us "For the Lord gives wisdom; from His mouth come knowledge and understanding." Each situation is unique, and God may prompt us to take a specific course of action or provide insights tailored to our circumstances. Trusting in the Lord's leading as we apply the wisdom gained from godly counsel is of utmost importance.

Scripture References

The Value of Wise Counsel
Proverbs 15:22

The Importance of the Source of Counsel
Psalm 111:10 + Proverbs 13:20

Approach to Seeking Counsel
James 1:5 + Proverbs 19:20

Ensuring Alignment with God's Word
Acts 17:11

God as the Ultimate Source of Wisdom
Proverbs 2:6

Challenge

Take a moment to pray and ask God about some of the people you have chosen to trust with advice and council. Write down what you feel God is saying. Is He revealing someone else or warning you about one of your choices? Make sure to write down how He guides you below.

RELATIONSHIP
... and ...
FAMILY

ONENESS

God made women for men after He saw that being alone was not good for man. She was formed out of man's ribs and was called woman. The Bible says that this is why a man leaves his father and mother and is united to his wife, and they become one flesh. Therefore, what God has joined together, let no one separate.

It is important to remember that you and your wife are one, especially when facing issues and conflicts in your marriage. Often, married couples fight face to face instead of shoulder to shoulder. You are both on the same team. Building a strong connection with your wife is the foundation of a healthy and successful marriage. Once you have developed this unity with your wife, you can tackle difficult decisions such as dealing with in-laws, parents, relatives, and children.

Oneness is built through trust, respect, and communication. It is something that will grow and develop with the more effort and time that is poured into it. The Trinity is a perfect example of oneness: God the Father, Jesus the Son, and the Holy Spirit. As each aspect of God functions differently, they all makeup God's Trinity.

Remember that your oneness with your wife is a sacred bond that should never be broken. This bond should be nurtured and protected, as it is a reflection of God's love for us. Once you have developed this unity with your wife, you can tackle difficult decisions within your marriage and stand strong so the enemy cannot cause division between you. A cord of three strands is not easily broken.

Scripture References

Origin and Purpose of Marriage
Genesis 2:18, 21-24

The Sacred Unity of Marriage
Mark 10:7-9

Facing Conflicts Together
Ecclesiastes 4:12

Oneness Through Trust, Respect, and Communication
1 Peter 3:7 + Ephesians 4:2-3

The Trinity as a Symbol of Unity
Matthew 28:19 + 2 Corinthians 13:14

Challenge

Think about some challenges you are facing right now. Write them down below, and then take a moment to share them with your spouse. Write down your spouse's challenges next to yours, and then pray for them daily.

PARENTS & IN-LAWS

Marriage is a sacred union, and when two individuals come together in matrimony, they bring with them their unique upbringing, traditions, and customs. Combining families can be challenging, but it is important to remember that the marriage between a man and a woman creates a new family, and it is their responsibility to build it according to God's plan. Once you are married, your wife and your kids are your first priority. Not your parents or in-laws.

As you navigate through the complexities of merging two families, remember that change is inevitable. Old traditions can be modified, new ones can be created, and some may need to be discarded altogether. My spouse and I got rid of celebrating Halloween. I was brought up with the understanding that it was an evil holiday while my wife was raised believing it was just for fun. It's important to communicate openly and honestly with your spouse about what works for both of you and what doesn't. Through prayer and discernment, you can come to an agreement and make decisions together that will strengthen your bond.

Remember, you are one now. Your family unit takes precedence over any other relationship or attachment from your past. When discussing family matters with others, always support and uplift your spouse. Be each other's advocate and work together to address any challenges that arise. Stand up for each other and stay in unity. Require respect for your spouse from your family. Let nothing come between you and your spouse, for what God has joined together, let no one separate.

Scripture References

Marriage as a Sacred Union
Genesis 2:24

Embracing Change and Building New Traditions
Isaiah 43:19

Communication and Agreement in Marriage
Amos 3:3

The Primacy of the Marital Bond
Mark 10:7-9

Challenge

Think about your parents and your in-laws. Are they too involved in specific aspects of your relationship? Write down each thing that comes to mind. Take some time to address each point with your husband, and remember to listen to what he has to say.

BAD INFLUENCES

In the Bible, it is clear that marriage is a sacred union between a husband and wife that should be protected from outside influences. It is common to encounter family members or others who believe they have a say in the decision-making process of your marriage. However, as a couple, it is essential to set boundaries and make it clear that your marriage is between you and your spouse.

Prayer is a powerful tool in seeking guidance and making decisions for your marriage. By seeking God's will, you can gain clarity and unity in your choices as a couple. Once you and your spouse agree on a decision, approach the person with love, kindness, and firmness.

Fasting is also a powerful way to seek God's guidance and wisdom in particularly difficult situations. The Bible encourages fasting as a means of drawing closer to God and seeking His will in our lives.

Remember, your marriage is a sacred union ordained by God, and your responsibility is to protect and cherish it. Seek His guidance and wisdom in making decisions for your marriage, and don't allow outside influences to sway your decisions.

Scripture References

Sacredness of Marriage
Genesis 2:24 + Mark 10:8-9

Setting Boundaries in Marriage
Proverbs 4:23 + Ephesians 5:31

Prayer and Decision Making
Philippians 4:6-7 + James 1:5

The Role of Fasting in Seeking Wisdom
Matthew 6:16-18 + Joel 2:12

Upholding the Integrity of Marriage
Hebrews 13:4 + Malachi 2:14-16

Challenge

Take a moment to think about all of your friends and her friends. Do any of these friends have an unhealthy influence in your relationship? Write down each one that comes to mind, and take some time to discuss them with your spouse.

SOUL
TIES

IDENTIFYING SOUL TIES

In the faith journey, it is essential to address our past to move forward. Before embarking on a new chapter with your spouse and starting a family, engaging in self-reflection concerning past relationships is crucial. Discussing past relationships and experiences can foster trust and confidence in your spouse.

It is essential to recognize that intimacy involves sharing the innermost parts of oneself with another person. It entails vulnerability and inviting someone to see into your heart and soul. God designed intimacy primarily for marriage, but it is possible to have deep emotional connections with parents, mentors, or leaders–relationships where you open your heart and soul to them, allowing them to shape you. Such connections can be healthy and enriching.

However, when referring to soul ties, we are addressing unhealthy relationships. These are relationships where you have been intimate with individuals who have manipulated or betrayed the sacred bond. Unfortunately, such situations occur more frequently than we realize, whether it is a spiritual mentor in the church or a family member whose motives have been compromised. In these cases, it is vital to seek God's guidance and ask Him to sever these ties.

Additionally, we must consider past sexual relationships. If you have engaged in sexual activity in the past, there is a strong likelihood of having a lingering connection, a tie, with that person. This is because God designed sex to unite husband and wife, bringing them closer together. It is an act where two souls become one in spirit.

If you find yourself in this situation, it is crucial to evaluate yourself honestly. Ask yourself: Do the people I have been intimately involved with in the past still affect me today? Do their actions or opinions continue to influence my thoughts and decisions? These are signs that you have not fully dealt with the tie you have with these individuals.

Scripture References

Self-Reflection and Addressing the Past
Psalm 139:23-24

The Depth of Intimacy
Proverbs 27:19

Understanding Unhealthy 'Soul Ties'
1 Corinthians 6:16-17

The Spiritual Significance of Sexual Relationships
Genesis 2:24

Evaluating and Healing Past Ties
Philippians 3:13-14 + James 5:16

Challenge

Write down the names of people who still affect you and invade your thoughts. Then pray and ask God to reveal any more people you forgot, and write them down.

DEALING WITH SOUL TIES

If you have read the previous section and sense that you may have formed soul ties or feel uncertain about it. Begin by listing everyone you believe you may have a soul tie with. Your spouse deserves a partner free from any lingering connections to past relationships. The good news is that the blood of Jesus covers it all. Now, applying His forgiveness to this sin is up to you.

Start by reviewing your list and seeking God's guidance on severing unhealthy ties with each person. Allow the Holy Spirit to direct you toward the appropriate course of action. The steps you take may be radical, such as leaving a church, or challenging, like confronting someone you once admired. However, remember that this process is about your future and healing.

After prayer, the next step involves taking tangible actions to sever the connection. If it is an ongoing relationship that is unhealthy, it may be time to end it and explain to the person their wrongdoing and why it is not acceptable. Remember that the Bible calls us to be peacemakers, which sometimes requires confrontation and discomfort. If it pertains to a past sexual relationship that still occupies your fantasies, pray to God, asking Him to remove all images from your mind and decide to never entertain such thoughts again. Perhaps there are physical reminders of a past relationship that you need to discard.

God may guide you in various ways, so listen attentively to the Holy Spirit's voice and address each person on your list individually. After dealing with each person, repent and ask God to break any soul ties you have with them. God desires to set us free.

Scripture References

Recognizing and Listing Soul Ties
Lamentations 3:40

Relying on Jesus' Redemption
1 John 1:7

Seeking God's Guidance in Severing Ties
John 14:26

Taking Concrete Actions Towards Healing
Matthew 5:9 + Philippians 4:8

Continuous Reflection and Evaluation
2 Corinthians 13:5

Challenge

Take action by completing the steps in the teaching. Write down each person's name below and what action you took to break the soul tie next to each person.

SEX

IN

... *Marriage* ...

GOD'S GIFT OF SEX

As followers of Christ, we know that sex is a gift from God. Unfortunately, the world often distorts this truth and feeds us lies that sex is dirty or impure. This is likely because sex is frequently misused outside of God's intended purpose, such as in cases of sexual abuse or outside of marriage. Tragically, our culture has become saturated with sexualization, affecting both women and men and making it difficult to discern God's plan for sex.

Our society constantly tempts us with images and messages that blur the lines of what sex truly is. But God created us as sexual beings with a natural desire for physical intimacy, which is beautiful and right within the confines of His purpose for marriage.

The Bible has no specific limitations on what is sexually permissible between a husband and a wife. However, the Bible does instruct us to honor our spouses and to offer our bodies to one another. It's essential to consider the comfort and willingness of your partner when exploring new sexual activities.

Communication is vital in maintaining a healthy sexual relationship with your spouse. It's essential to keep the conversation open and honest and to respect each other's boundaries and desires. By honoring one another, we can enjoy the beautiful gift of sex as God intended.

Scripture References

Sex as a Gift from God
Genesis 2:24-25

Cultural Distortions
Romans 12:2

Freedom Within Boundaries
Romans 12:10

Importance of Communication
Ephesians 4:25-27

Mutual Respect and Consent
Philippians 2:3-4

Challenge

Write down any sexual desire that excites you. If it's within the confines of marriage between you and your husband, then it's permissible. Go over the list with your husband and discuss each item so that you both know each other's expectations.

ACTIVE SEX LIFE

So many men and women today are sexually frustrated. Sometimes a spouse can unknowingly deprive their partner sexually. Everyone's sexual drive is different, and it's essential to have this conversation with your husband so you both have clear expectations on how to fulfill each other's desires.

In 1 Corinthians 7:5 the Bible tells us to not deprive one another, except perhaps by agreement for a limited time, that you may devote yourself to prayer; but then come together again, so that Satan may not tempt you because of your lack of self-control. This scripture explains precisely why we should not keep sex from our partners. We are responsible to our partners to fulfill their needs to not only help them with any sexual frustration but to also protect your home from spiritual attack in the form of temptation.

Regular sex should be a staple in your marriage. So many marriages fail due to infidelity and it starts with sexual frustration, which leads to sexual desire being fed to us from our culture. The the enemy waits for an opening to attack while your partner is weak. Don't give the devil this satisfaction. Keep your partner satisfied.

There are times when abstinence is okay within a godly marriage and that is when both husband and wife have agreed upon it for a short period. Mainly for a time of prayer and fasting, there are situations where spouses may choose to sacrifice themselves for the sanctification and glory of God. However, in Ephesians 5 husbands are taught to care for their wives as their own bodies, emphasizing nurturing and cherishing. This guidance can apply to periods of abstinence, like after childbirth, where self-control and understanding are important.

Ultimately, a healthy and satisfying sexual relationship within marriage is a gift from God, designed to strengthen our bond with our spouse and protect us from the enemy's attacks. By honoring our partner's needs and desires, we celebrate God's plan for our marriage and create a foundation of love, trust, and mutual respect.

Scripture References

Sexual Frustration, Regular Intimacy, Spiritual Attacks, and Abstinence
"Do not deprive each other except perhaps by mutual consent and for a time, so that you may devote yourselves to prayer. Then come together again so that Satan will not tempt you because of your lack of self-control."
1 Corinthians 7:5

Sexual Intimacy as a Gift from God
Genesis 2:24

Challenge

Take a moment to think about how often you desire sex. Write it down below and then discuss it with your spouse.

DUTY SEX

As followers of Christ, we are called to honor our marriage and our spouse. God's plan for marriage includes physical intimacy between a husband and wife. It is not something that should be neglected or taken lightly. In 1 Corinthians 7:3-5, the Bible instructs us not to deprive each other sexually except for a limited time to devote ourselves to prayer. This shows us that sexual intimacy is an essential part of marriage and that we should not neglect it.

However, if sex stops being enjoyable and is treated like a duty or obligation, this is a problem. If it becomes a duty to one spouse, they may avoid having sex because of the pressure to perform something they do not want. This makes it harder for the other spouse who longs for physical intimacy, worrying about whether their needs will be met.

You need to be open and honest with each other so that you both feel safe and respected. Work together to create a sexual relationship that meets the needs of both you and your spouse.

If you are in a place where you feel sex is an obligation, instead of focusing on performing out of guilt or duty, you should focus on reconnecting with your spouse and your own sexual desires for them. You can ask God to restore your passion for your spouse. He is a good Father who knows our needs and desires, and He made sex for us to enjoy within our marriage. Be vulnerable, and remember there are other ways to connect that can grow your intimacy and trust aside from being physical.

A marriage cannot thrive without physical intimacy. As we seek to honor God and our spouse, let us strive to maintain a healthy sexual relationship within our marriage and work through any obstacles.

Scripture References

Marital Oneness in Christ
Mark 10:8 + Ephesians 5:31

Significance of Physical Intimacy
1 Corinthians 7:3-5

Respecting Boundaries and Feelings
Philippians 2:3-4 + Romans 12:10

Patience and Sacrifice in Marriage
Colossians 3:12-13 + 1 Corinthians 13:4-7

Challenge

Think about whether or not you feel safe and comfortable talking about sex and engaging in sex with your spouse. Write your thoughts down below and then discuss it with your spouse.

MANIPULATIVE SEX

In marriage, the Bible instructs husbands to have authority over their wives, including their bodies. Husbands are called to love their wives just as Christ loves the church, and wives are instructed to honor and respect their husbands. However, this does not mean that a husband can use this authority to abuse his wife sexually and vice versa. We must always strive to treat our spouses with love, respect, and dignity.

In a godly marriage, using sex as a means of control or manipulation over your spouse is wrong. Deceit, or using others for personal gain, goes against God's will for our lives. Marriage is a covenant between two people and is meant to be based on love, trust, and mutual respect. Using sex to gain control over your spouse is a tactic of the enemy, and it goes against everything God desires for our marriages. You should never use sex as a tool to get what you want from your spouse, and you should never withhold sex as a punishment. It can also be manipulative when one spouse makes the other feel guilty for saying no.

As Christians, we are called to repent and turn away from our sins. If you have been using sex to manipulate or control your spouse, it is important to acknowledge this sin and surrender it to Jesus. Confess your wrongdoing to your spouse, seek forgiveness from them, and make a commitment to change your ways. Remember that God's plan for marriage is for both partners to be united in love and intimacy, not for one to use sex as a tool for manipulation.

You should both feel safe enough to talk about sex and feel safe with each other while being intimate. When you don't feel safe, it is hard to surrender and be vulnerable with your spouse, let alone enjoy physical intimacy. Sex should not be a taboo topic in your marriage. You need to communicate with your spouse and be open and honest with each other. You can find a way to honor one another while both feeling safe and respected when it comes to physical intimacy.

Scripture References

Sexual Manipulation as Sin
1 Thessalonians 4:3-6

Decet and Using Other for Personal Gain
Proverbs 26:24-26 + 2 Corinthians 4:2

Mutual Authority in Marriage
1 Corinthians 7:4

Husbands' Role: Love and Respect
Ephesians 5:25-28

Wives' Role: Honor and Respect
Ephesians 5:22-24

Challenge

Have you ever been a victim or engaged in sexual abuse in any way? Have you ever used sex as a tool to manipulate, or do you feel your spouse does? Write your experience, and take time to talk through it with your wife.

Overcoming LUST ISSUES

PORNOGRAPHY

Addressing the topic of pornography from a biblical perspective requires careful consideration of God's design for human relationships and the principles outlined in Scripture. While the Bible does not explicitly mention pornography, we can apply its teachings to understand its impact on individuals and marriages.

Pornography involves the consumption of explicit sexual material that is intended to arouse sexual desire and stimulate lustful thoughts. The Bible makes it clear that lustful thoughts and actions are sinful. Jesus Himself stated that even looking at another person with lustful intent is equivalent to committing adultery in the heart (Matthew 5:27-28).

Engaging in pornography contradicts God's call for purity, self-control, and the sanctity of the marriage covenant. It objectifies individuals, distorts the true meaning of intimacy, and undermines the trust and emotional connection within a marital relationship. Discovering a spouse's involvement in pornography can lead to feelings of betrayal, inadequacy, and insecurity.

Pornography portrays distorted and unrealistic views of human sexuality, often promoting harmful and degrading behaviors. It fosters a mindset prioritizing self-gratification over the selfless love and mutual respect that should characterize a healthy marital relationship. Furthermore, it can create an unhealthy dependence on artificial stimuli and hinder the development of genuine intimacy and emotional connection between spouses.

The Bible urges believers to guard their hearts and minds, recognizing that they are the wellspring of life (Proverbs 4:23). Consuming pornography pollutes one's thoughts, corrupts their understanding of God's design for sexuality, and creates a barrier in their relationship with God. It hinders spiritual growth and can lead to a cycle of guilt, shame, and addiction.

For those struggling with the temptation of pornography, seeking help and support is crucial. Confessing the struggle to God, seeking His forgiveness, support is crucial. Confessing the struggle to God, seeking His forgiveness, and relying on His strength can bring healing and restoration. Additionally, reaching out to a trusted spiritual mentor, participating in support groups, or seeking professional counseling can provide guidance, accountability, and practical tools for overcoming pornography addiction.

Within a marital context, discovering a spouse's involvement in pornography can be devastating. It is essential for couples to foster open and honest communication, seeking healing and reconciliation through God's grace. Professional counseling and pastoral guidance can provide valuable assistance in addressing the effects of pornography within a marriage, with a commitment to rebuilding trust and intimacy.

Pornography is a dangerous trap that can ensnare individuals and devastate their lives and relationships. Like a drug addiction, pornography often starts small but can escalate to more explicit and harmful content over time. It creates a cycle of dissatisfaction, driving individuals to seek more potent stimuli. This destructive path can lead some down the dark road of exploring illegal and immoral content. The consequences of such actions are severe and have far-reaching implications, not only for the individual but also their spouse and the sanctity of their marital bond.

Recognizing the addictive nature of pornography is crucial. Seeking help, healing, and the grace of God, along with the support of trusted individuals and resources, is essential for breaking free from its grip. By embracing God's design for purity, selflessness, and faithfulness in our thoughts and actions, we can honor Him, protect our marriages, and experience the fullness of the abundant life He has called us to.

Scripture References

Pornography and Sin
Matthew 5:27-28

Marital Trust and Emotional Connection
Ephesians 5:25-33

Cycle of Guilt, Shame, and Addiction
Proverbs 4:23

Seeking Help and Support
James 5:16

Dangerous Escalation
Romans 6:16

Restoration through God's Grace
1 John 1:9

Challenge

Use the space below to answer the following questions, and discuss your answers with your wife. Do you have a problem with pornography now, or in the past? Expand on this with your spouse (what kind, how long).

____

____

____

____

____

____

____

____

ADULTERY IN THE HEART

Adultery is a grave offense in the eyes of God and is clearly condemned throughout Scripture. However, it is important to recognize that adultery does not begin with physical acts alone; rather, it originates in the heart. Jesus Himself taught that "Everyone who looks at a woman with lustful intent has already committed adultery with her in his heart." in Matthew 5:28. This powerful statement reveals the root cause of adultery: the corrupt desires and thoughts that take root within us.

Adultery often starts subtly, with small compromises and thoughts that go against the covenant of marriage. It may begin with harmless interactions or seemingly innocent connections with someone other than your spouse. These interactions, if fueled by improper motives or desires, can open the door for temptation to enter our hearts. When we entertain lustful thoughts, fantasies, or emotional connections outside of marriage, we are stepping onto a dangerous path that can lead to destruction.

If left unchecked, these small compromises can grow into something much more significant. The seed of lust, when nurtured, can take root and flourish, gradually consuming our thoughts and desires. It can lead to secret communications, hidden meetings, and a growing emotional attachment to someone other than your spouse. The progression from lustful thoughts to actual physical adultery can be devastating and has the potential to cause irreparable damage to the marital bond.

Adultery not only breaks the trust and commitment between spouses, but it also fractures the spiritual and emotional connection established by God. It destroys the sacred covenant of marriage, which is intended to reflect the union between Christ and the Church. Adultery can bring about pain, heartache, and shattered dreams, leading to feelings of betrayal, guilt, and shame.

To prevent adultery from taking hold in our hearts and marriages, we must be vigilant and guard our hearts against the allure of temptation. We are called to cultivate purity, faithfulness, and self-control in our thoughts and actions. This begins with renewing our minds and aligning our desires with God's Word. We must actively resist the temptations that come our way and flee from situations that could potentially lead us astray.

Should we find ourselves struggling with impure thoughts or desires, we must humbly turn to God for forgiveness, grace, and strength. Confession, repentance, and a renewed commitment to honoring the marriage covenant are crucial steps towards healing and restoration. In seeking reconciliation, we must be willing to face the consequences of our actions, seek forgiveness from our spouse, and take the necessary steps to rebuild trust and intimacy.

Let us remember that God's desire for our marriages is one of faithfulness, love, and unity. By guarding our hearts, renewing our minds, and relying on the guidance of the Holy Spirit, we can uphold the sanctity of marriage and experience the abundant blessings that come from honoring God's design for marital fidelity.

Scripture References

Adultery and Lust
Matthew 5:28

The Sacredness of Marriage
Mark 10:9

Guarding against Temptation
Ephesians 6:10-18

Confession and Repentance
1 John 1:9

Challenge

Do you struggle with impure thoughts? Think about your time on social media, TV or the people you see throughout your day. Write down a list of things you do, or apps you use that fuel these thoughts and actions you can take to reduce or remove the triggers for those thoughts.

WORLDLY CULTURE

In today's world, we are bombarded with messages that exploit and manipulate our desires, often using lust as a means to draw us in or sell us things. Advertisements, media, and entertainment industries frequently portray images and narratives that fuel lustful thoughts and fantasies, presenting them as desirable and normal. The world promotes a culture that celebrates instant gratification, objectification, and the pursuit of pleasure above all else.

However, as believers, we are called to resist the temptations of the world and align our lives with God's Word. It is crucial to recognize the dangers of succumbing to the world's seductive messages and to guard our hearts and minds against the influences that lead to lustful desires.

In the context of marriage, lust can have a detrimental effect on the spouse. It creates a divide in the emotional and spiritual connection between husband and wife, leading to feelings of betrayal, insecurity, and inadequacy. The world's portrayal of lust as a normative behavior undermines the sacredness of marriage, distorting the true meaning of intimacy and love.

The world's use of lust as a marketing tool or a means to manipulate our desires can contribute to a cycle of dissatisfaction and discontentment within the marital relationship. When one partner becomes entangled in the web of lust, seeking fulfillment outside the marriage, it hinders the growth of a deep and meaningful connection based on love, respect, and selflessness.

To combat the destructive influence of lust in the world, believers are called to cultivate purity and self-control. We must be discerning and aware of the messages surrounding us, guarding our minds and hearts against the influences leading to lustful desires. By immersing ourselves in God's Word, seeking His guidance, and relying on the power of the Holy Spirit, we can resist the temptations of the world and embrace the biblical principles of love, fidelity, and selflessness in our marital relationships. Have you ever heard the saying you are what you eat? Well, the same applies to your thoughts. Open communication and transparency within the marital relationship are crucial in addressing the effects of lust. Spouses should be able to discuss their struggles, fears, and temptations with one another, creating an atmosphere of love, understanding, and forgiveness. By fostering an environment of trust and vulnerability, couples can support each other in overcoming the lure of lust and grow together in purity.

Our focus should be aligning our lives with God's Word and resisting the world's temptations. By cultivating purity, honoring the sanctity of marriage, and prioritizing our spouse's emotional and spiritual well-being, we can build strong and fulfilling marriages that reflect God's design for intimacy and love.

Let us be mindful of the world's attempts to draw us into the web of lust and instead fix our eyes on Jesus, seeking His guidance and strength to resist the allure of the world. In doing so, we can experience the true joy and fulfillment that comes from a God-honoring marriage built on love, respect, and fidelity.

Scripture References

Lust and Sinful Desires
1 John 2:16

Guarding our Hearts and Minds
Proverbs 4:23

Resisting Worldly Temptations
Romans 12:2

Purity and Self-control
Galatians 5:22-23

Challenge

Think about what you have seen lately on advertisements, media, streaming services and fashion. Write down all the triggers that fuel lustful thoughts. Share your triggers with your wife along with your thoughts on each one. Have an open discussion on how they effect your marriage and how you can combat them together.

MASTURBATION

The topic of masturbation from a biblical viewpoint calls for careful thought, and guidance from the Holy Spirit. Even though the Bible doesn't talk about masturbation directly, we can surely look to its principles to help us form a better understanding.

First and foremost, it is important to acknowledge that lustful thoughts are considered a sin according to the teachings of the Bible. Jesus emphasized the seriousness of this matter, stating that whoever looks at another person with lustful intent has already committed adultery in their heart (Matthew 5:27-28). Lust objectifies others and undermines the sanctity of human relationships.

When considering masturbation, examining the motives and thoughts accompanying this act is crucial. If masturbation involves entertaining lustful thoughts for someone other than your spouse, it contradicts biblical principles. The Bible calls us to purity, self-control, and fidelity in our thoughts and actions.

However, it is worth noting that the Bible does not prohibit sexual desire or attraction within the context of marriage. In fact, the Song of Solomon portrays the beautiful and passionate love shared between a husband and wife. Within the marriage covenant, it is natural and appropriate for spouses to desire and enjoy one another intimately.

When addressing masturbation within marriage, it is essential to distinguish between lustful thoughts and the healthy expression of sexual desire for one's spouse. Lustful thoughts involve objectifying others and seeking self-gratification at the expense of God's design for sexual intimacy. In contrast, desiring and cherishing your spouse within the boundaries of the marital relationship is a God-given blessing.

It is crucial to seek the guidance of the Holy Spirit when considering these matters. The Holy Spirit convicts us of sin, guides us in truth, and empowers us to live in obedience to God's Word. Regular prayer, study of Scripture, and seeking counsel from wise and trusted spiritual mentors can help you discern-God's will for your unique circumstances.

Remember, as believers, we are called to love, honor, and respect our spouses. This includes nurturing a healthy, intimate relationship where both partners feel cherished and satisfied. By cultivating open and honest communication, embracing self-control, and honoring the sanctity of marriage, we can navigate the topic of masturbation in a way that aligns with biblical principles and strengthens the bond between spouses.

Our responsibility is to guard our hearts and minds, seeking to glorify God in all aspects of our lives, including our thoughts and actions regarding sexual intimacy.

Scripture References

Lustful Intent and Adultery in the Heart
Matthew 5:27-28

Guidance from the Holy Spirit
John 14:26 + John 14:16

Purity, Self-control, and Fidelity
1 Thessalonians 4:3-5 + Galatians 5:22-23

Marriage and Sexual Intimacy
Proverbs 5:18-19 + 1 Corinthians 7:5

Guarding Hearts and Minds
Proverbs 4:23 + 2 Corinthians 10:5

Challenge

Write down whether or not you masturbate, and if it's accompanied by lustful thoughts. Discuss this with your spouse and come up with a plan for moving forward.

GROUNDS FOR DIVORCE

Marriage is a sacred covenant established by God, designed to reflect the selfless love, commitment, and unity between Christ and the Church. In this divine union, both spouses are called to honor and cherish one another, nurturing a relationship that withstands the tests of time. However, the reality is that marriages can face significant challenges and hardships, leading some to consider the possibility of divorce.

The Bible addresses the issue of divorce, and while it acknowledges that marital difficulties may arise, it sets a high standard for what constitutes grounds for divorce. Jesus, in His teachings, affirms the sanctity of marriage and emphasizes that divorce was never intended to be a casual or easy option. He states "Therefore what God has joined together, let no one separate." in Matthew 19:6. The Bible upholds the lifelong commitment of marriage, encouraging couples to seek reconciliation, forgiveness, and restoration rather than resorting to divorce.

Adultery is one specific circumstance that the Bible recognizes as grounds for divorce. Jesus states "I tell you that anyone who divorces his wife, except for sexual immorality, and marries another woman commits adultery" in Matthew 19:9. Adultery involves a breach of trust and the breaking of the marital covenant. It inflicts deep wounds and can cause painful damage to the relationship.

However, it is important to note that even in the case of adultery, forgiveness and reconciliation are encouraged. The Bible consistently emphasizes the power of forgiveness and the restoration of relationships. God desires couples to work through the pain, seek healing, and rebuild trust, ultimately restoring the marriage to its intended state of unity and love.

It recognizes that marriages face various challenges, such as abuse, abandonment, and severe, unrepentant sin. In such cases, seeking professional help, guidance, and wise counsel is crucial to navigating the situation's complexities. The primary focus should always be pursuing reconciliation, restoration, and honoring God's design for marriage.

As followers of Christ, we are called to emulate His sacrificial love and forgiveness. The Bible teaches us to forgive one another, just as God in Christ forgave us (Ephesians 4:32). It urges us to bear with one another and to be humble, patient, and kind in our interactions (Colossians 3:12-14). By embracing these principles, we can cultivate an atmosphere of grace and mercy within our marriages.

Marriage is a journey that requires dedication, selflessness, and a steadfast commitment to working through challenges. While divorce may seem like an easy way out in moments of difficulty, the Bible encourages us to lean on God's strength, seek reconciliation, and strive to restore the beauty and unity of our marriages. Through prayer, communication, counseling, and reliance on the Holy Spirit, we can overcome obstacles and experience the redemptive power of God's love within our marriages.

Scripture References

Sacredness and Commitment of Marriage
Matthew 19:6

Jesus on Divorce and Adultery
Matthew 19:9

Forgiveness and Reconciliation
Ephesians 4:32 + Matthew 5:23-24

Characteristics of Love and Dealing with Challenges
Colossians 3:13 + 1 Corinthians 13:4-5

Reliance on the Holy Spirit and Prayer
Galtions 5:22-23 + Philippians 4:6

Challenge

How did the relationship between your parents affect you? Did you grow up in a broken home? Write down your answers below and how you feel about it. Take time to discuss this with your wife.

ALL
• • • About • • •
MONEY

GIVING ALL YOU HAVE

In the sacred bond of marriage, husbands, and wives are called to support and care for one another in all aspects of life, including managing finances. The Bible teaches us about the importance of providing for and ensuring the financial well-being of our spouse, particularly for the husband as the head of the household.

Pooling your financial resources in a joint account fosters transparency, trust, and a sense of shared ownership. This reflects the biblical principle of oneness in marriage. Together, as one flesh, you embark on a journey of financial stewardship, making decisions collectively and supporting each other in abundance and scarcity.

Scripture further emphasizes the husband's role as a provider, recognizing his responsibility to diligently work and make provisions for his family. The Apostle Paul writes "But if anyone does not provide for his relatives, and especially for members of his household, he has denied the faith and is worse than an unbeliever." in 1 Timothy 5:8. This verse underscores the significance of the husband's role in ensuring there is enough money to meet the family's needs.

However, it is essential to note that this arrangement does not negate the need for joint decision-making and open communication. Both spouses should be involved in financial discussions, actively setting financial goals and making decisions together. The husband's role as the provider does not mean that the wife is excluded from financial matters, but rather that she can find reassurance in her husband's commitment to ensuring their financial stability.

When you view your earnings as shared rather than individual, it fosters a sense of unity. It reduces the temptation for financial secrets or selfishness. Understand that any income earned belongs to both of you, reinforcing the biblical principle of selflessness and sacrificial love within your marriage. This shared perspective encourages open communication and fosters a spirit of generosity, where resources are used to benefit your family and to honor God.

Families must cultivate a spirit of wisdom and diligence in their financial stewardship. This includes budgeting, saving, and making wise decisions to meet the family's needs. Seeking God's guidance and being good stewards of the resources entrusted to them helps husbands fulfill their role as providers and protectors of their families.

When financial challenges arise, couples need to support and encourage one another. Together, they can seek God's guidance, explore solutions, and make necessary adjustments to navigate difficult times. Mutual respect, trust, and understanding are vital in maintaining a healthy and harmonious financial partnership.

Above all, the Bible calls husbands and wives to approach finances with selflessness, generosity, and contentment. It reminds us that our ultimate trust should be in God, the true provider of all our needs. By working together, supporting one another, and seeking God's wisdom, husbands and wives can create a financial environment that fosters unity, peace, and the family's well-being.

Scripture References

Oneness in Marriage
Genesis 2:24

The Husband's Role as a Provider
1 Timothy 5:8

Financial Stewardship and Wisdom
Proverbs 21:5 + Proverbs 13:22

Trust in God as Provider
Philippians 4:19 + Jeremiah 29:11

Contentment
Philippians 4:11 + 1 Timothy 6:6

Challenge

Take a moment to discuss opening a joint checking account with your spouse. Schedule a date with him as well as a bank and a time, and commit to it by writing it down below. Also, discuss how you will manage your account and who is responsible for what.

HOW TO HANDLE DEBT

Debt is a common financial challenge many couples face, encompassing mortgages, student loans, credit card debt, and car loans. However, the Bible offers valuable principles and guidance on how couples can approach and manage debt in a responsible and God-honoring manner. Let's explore some biblical perspectives on debt management.

The Bible encourages us to exercise wisdom and discernment regarding debt, as stated in Proverbs 22:7: "The rich rule over the poor, and the borrower is slave to the lender." This verse reminds us of the potential pitfalls of excessive debt and the burden it can place on our lives. Couples should avoid unnecessary or impulsive debt, making informed decisions based on careful consideration and financial prudence.

Scripture teaches the importance of living within our means and being content with what we have. In 1 Timothy 6:6-8, it says "But godliness with contentment is great gain." For we brought nothing into the world, and we can take nothing out of it. But if we have food and clothing, we will be content with that. By adopting a mindset of contentment and avoiding a lifestyle of excessive borrowing, couples can reduce the risk of falling into unmanageable debt.

The Bible emphasizes the importance of integrity and honoring our commitments, including our financial obligations. Psalm 37:21 states "The wicked borrow and do not repay, but the righteous give generously." Couples should prioritize making timely payments and fulfilling their financial responsibilities. This includes honoring loan agreements, paying bills promptly, and meeting financial obligations with diligence and integrity.

Seeking wise counsel and advice is crucial when it comes to managing debt. Couples should consider consulting financial advisors, seeking guidance from trusted mentors, or involving a qualified professional to help them develop a debt management plan. Seeking counsel can provide valuable insights, perspectives, and strategies to navigate debt wisely.

Couples should consider consulting financial advisors, seeking guidance from trusted mentors, or involving a qualified professional to help them develop a debt management plan. Seeking counsel can provide valuable insights, perspectives, and strategies to navigate debt wisely.

The Bible encourages us to be diligent in repaying our debts. Couples should prioritize debt repayment by developing a realistic budget, allocating funds specifically for debt reduction, and making consistent and disciplined payments. Couples can experience financial freedom and peace of mind by taking proactive steps to reduce debt.

A biblical perspective on debt management reminds us to trust in God's provision and guidance. Philippians 4:19 assures us "And my God will meet all your needs according to the riches of his glory in Christ Jesus." By seeking God's wisdom, praying for guidance, and trusting in His provision, couples can find strength and peace amidst their financial challenges. Trusting in God's faithfulness enables couples to navigate debt with hope and confidence.

Managing debt can be daunting, but by applying these biblical principles, couples can approach debt management with wisdom, responsibility, and faith. By avoiding unwise debt, not making hasty financial decisions, living within means, honoring commitments, seeking counsel, prioritizing debt repayment, and trusting in God's provision, couples can lay a foundation for financial freedom and cultivate a healthy and God-honoring relationship with money. Remember, the journey towards debt freedom requires discipline, perseverance, and reliance on God's guidance and grace.

Scripture References

Wisdom and Discernment in Handling Debt
Proverbs 22:7

Living Within Our Means and Contentment
1 Timothy 6:6-8

Honoring Financial Commitments
Psalm 37:21

Seeking Wise Counsel and Advice
Proverbs 15:22

Diligence in Repaying Debts
Romans 13:8

Trusting in God's Provision
Philippians 4:19

Challenge

List your debt in the space below and then share it with your husband. Make a plan with your spouse to pay off the debt together and discuss ways to stay debt-free moving forward.

SETTING EXPECTATIONS

Within a marriage, spouses often have different spending preferences and lifestyles. It is crucial to find a balance through compromise. If one spouse has expensive taste, but the income doesn't support it, it is wise to seek affordable alternatives that align with the available resources. Cultivating contentment with what one has and living within means fosters financial harmony.

Financial disparities can exist within couples, with one spouse earning more than the other. Often, one spouse might spend quicker while the other likes to save. However, it's important to remember that money should not create a power dynamic or sense of entitlement in the relationship. Instead of viewing income as separate, it should be seen as shared resources. Both spouses are equal partners, regardless of their financial contributions. Unity and teamwork should prevail, ensuring that financial decisions are made together, respecting each other's input.

Couples should recognize and appreciate the different roles and contributions each brings to the family, including the valuable work of a stay-at-home parent. Financial decisions should be made with mutual respect and acknowledgment of each spouse's sacrifices and efforts. It is essential to give equal weight to the opinions and desires of both partners, regardless of their financial status. Ultimately, it is the husband's responsibility to make the final decision.

Financial infidelity, such as maintaining secret bank accounts or credit cards, erodes trust within a marriage. Honesty and transparency in financial matters are essential. Spouses should openly communicate about their financial activities, including any additional accounts or debts they may have. Fostering an environment of trust and openness enables couples to work together towards shared financial goals and rebuild any lost confidence. Unmet expectations often lead to disappointment and conflict in marriage. It is essential to approach financial goals with realism and patience. Recognize that financial success is a journey that may require time, effort, and sacrifice. Avoid comparing your situation to societal norms or unrealistic expectations. Instead, prioritize financial stability, make wise decisions, and work together to achieve shared aspirations over time.

By applying these biblical principles and insights, couples can navigate the complexities of financial expectations within marriage. Through compromise, unity, honesty, contentment, and patience, couples can strengthen their financial bond and create a solid foundation for a harmonious and fulfilling marital relationship. Remember, the shared journey and mutual support matter as you work together to build a prosperous and loving life.

Scripture References

Balancing Spending Preferences and Lifestyles
1 Timothy 6:7-8

Acknowledging Different Roles and Contributions
1 Peter 4:10

Honesty and Transparency in Financial Matters
Ephesians 4:25

Approaching Financial Goals with Realism and Patience
Galatians 6:9

Challenge

Think about whether you are a spender or a saver. Write down your answer along with all your bank accounts and credit cards. Then, write down your spending habits and must-have items. Share your answers with your husband and discuss your similarities and differences.

TITHE, OFFERING & GIFTS

Tithing, offering, and giving gifts are essential aspects of biblical stewardship and worship, expressing our gratitude to God. These practices have been emphasized in the Old and New Testaments, providing insights into their relevance today.

In the Old Testament, tithing meant giving God one-tenth of our income or resources. This practice, mentioned in passages like Leviticus 27:30 and Malachi 3:10, primarily supported the Levites who served in the temple and had no land inheritance. It also helped meet the needs of the poor and facilitated worship. Tithing allowed God's people to acknowledge His provision and demonstrate their trust in Him.

Alongside tithing, the Old Testament highlighted the importance of voluntary offerings and freewill gifts. These were given beyond the required tithe and supported various purposes like sustaining the priesthood, maintaining the temple, and carrying out charitable works. Such offerings were acts of gratitude, worship, and obedience to God. Proverbs also emphasizes the blessings that come from being a cheerful giver.

In the New Testament, giving extends beyond strict adherence to a specific tithe percentage. Acts 2:44-45 and Acts 4:32-35 illustrate the sacrificial giving and sharing of possessions within the early Christian community, ensuring that no one lacked what they needed. These passages exemplify the spirit of generosity and selflessness among the early believers.

Although the New Testament doesn't explicitly command tithing, it emphasizes principles for giving. The apostle Paul encourages believers to give generously, cheerfully, and purposefully. In 2 Corinthians 9:6-7, Paul writes, "Remember this: Whoever sows sparingly will also reap sparingly, and whoever sows generously will also reap generously. Each of you should give what you have decided in your heart to give, not reluctantly or under compulsion, for God loves a cheerful giver." Giving is seen as an act of worship, faith, an expression of love for God and others, and a means to support ministry.

At the core of giving is the understanding that it goes beyond meeting financial obligations or fulfilling religious duties. Giving reflects our relationship with God and our knowledge of His grace. It acknowledges that everything we possess comes from God and belongs to Him. Through giving, we can participate in His work, experience the joy of blessing others, and demonstrate our faith and trust in His provision.

Practically applying these biblical principles to your life requires prayerful consideration. While tithing can serve as a helpful guideline, the focus should be on giving generously according to our means and as guided by the Holy Spirit. This may involve supporting the local church, contributing to missions, helping those in need, and engaging in acts of kindness and service. Giving should be done willingly, with a cheerful heart, without compulsion or guilt. Before giving, it's important to pray and seek guidance from the Holy Spirit on how much to give and how to allocate our resources wisely.

Understanding the principles behind these practices and engaging in them sincerely and prayerfully allows us to align our giving with God's heart and purposes. This enriches our relationship with Him and its a significant aspect of biblical stewardship.

Scripture References

Tithing in the Old Testament
Leviticus 27:30 + Malachi 3:10

Voluntary Offerings and Freewill Gifts in the Old Testament
Proverbs 3:9-10 + Proverbs 11:24

Generosity and Sharing in the New Testament
Acts 2:44-45

Principles of Giving in the New Testament
2 Corinthians 9:6-7

Challenge

Discuss how you plan on tithing. Is it a percent, do you pray for an amount, or do you give a specific amount each time? How about offerings and gifts? Write down your thoughts and share them with your husband. Discuss how you will give moving forward as a couple.

FINANCIAL PLANNING

Financial planning is an essential aspect of married life. The Bible offers principles and wisdom that can guide couples in creating a financial plan that aligns with God's purposes and brings harmony to their relationship.

Begin by seeking God's wisdom and guidance in your financial planning. Pray together as a couple, inviting God to be the center of your financial decisions. Acknowledge that all resources belong to Him and commit to honoring Him with your finances.

Discuss and establish shared financial goals as a couple. These goals may include saving for emergencies, paying off debts, planning for retirement, giving to charitable causes, and providing for your family's needs. Align your goals with biblical values and prioritize them based on their significance.

Create a budget that reflects your financial goals and priorities. Budgeting helps you track income and expenses, manage resources wisely, and avoid unnecessary debt. Consider biblical stewardship principles, such as living within your means, avoiding excessive borrowing, and being content with what you have.

Maintain open and transparent communication about finances with your spouse. Regularly discuss income, expenses, and financial decisions. Honesty and transparency build trust and unity in your financial journey.

Guard against the temptation of materialism and the pursuit of wealth for its own sake. Cultivate contentment and gratitude for what God has provided. Avoid excessive consumerism and focus on stewarding resources to fulfill God's purposes and bless others.

Develop a savings plan and set aside funds for emergencies, future needs, and long-term goals. Consider biblical principles of diligence, prudence, and wise stewardship when investing. Seek godly counsel and research investment options that align with biblical values. Make giving a priority in your financial plan. The Bible encourages believers to be generous and cheerful givers. Allocate a portion of your income for tithes, offerings, and charitable giving. "Trust in God's provision, knowing that whoever sows sparingly will also reap sparingly, and whoever sows bountifully will also reap bountifully."(2 Corinthians 9:6)

Periodically review and adjust your financial plan to accommodate income, expenses, and goals changes. Seek God's guidance and evaluate if your financial decisions are aligned with His will. Be flexible and willing to make necessary adjustments as circumstances evolve.

Consider seeking professional financial advice, such as from a Christian financial counselor or planner, especially when dealing with complex financial matters. Look for advisors who share your biblical values and principles.

Financial planning is not solely about accumulating wealth but about stewarding resources in a way that honors God and benefits others. By seeking His guidance, communicating openly, and applying biblical principles, couples can create a financial plan that brings unity, peace, and economic well-being to their marriage.

Scripture References

Seeking God's Guidance
James 1:5

Budgeting
Proverbs 21:5

Guard Against Materialism
Hebrews 13:5

Savings and Investments
Proverbs 21:20

Challenge

Create a weekly or monthly budget for your family with your wife. Make sure to include areas for not just expenses but also savings if possible.

FRUITFUL

and

RESPONSIBLE

PROTECTING YOUR INHERITANCE

The Bible instructs us to be fruitful and multiply, and it is my hope that you have plans to have children if you haven't already. The gift of having children is one of the most precious blessings bestowed upon us by God. As a father, I am profoundly honored and grateful that God has entrusted me to pastor and guide His children. It is true that this responsibility is not always easy; in fact, it often requires sacrificing our own desires because our flesh tends to resist sacrifice. However, it is also gratifying, and I fervently pray that God will bless us with more children.

Regarding children, God has entrusted us with these precious little ones to teach and mentor. This means we have a duty to protect them from the enemy's schemes. We should diligently pray for them, guide them with great care in today's culture, and raise them according to the ways of the Lord. Although it may seem challenging, considering that everything in our modern world diminishes our control over what our children eat, drink, see, hear, and read, we cannot use that as an excuse. We must do everything we can to safeguard the inheritance God has given us.

Every child is a blessing. It is an honor and such a big responsibility to be entrusted with. We are in charge of their needs, growth, and discipline. We have to be an example, not just with our words but with our actions. We also have to remember that our kids are arrows in our quiver. As parents, we are the bow that aims our children in which direction they will go. We need to remember not to protect them in the quiver forever but to prepare them to be launched into battle for the Kingdom of God.

Scripture References

Biblical Mandate to Be Fruitful and Multiply
Genesis 1:28

Children as a Blessing
Psalm 127:3

Training Our Children
Proverbs 22:6

Your Responsibility as a Spiritual Leader
1 Peter 5:2

Duty to Protect
Matthew 18:6

Challenge

Write down your thoughts on having children. Include a mission statement and a goal for your family. Share your thoughts with your spouse and work together on your mission statement and goals.

FAMILY IS YOUR FIRST MINISTRY

God has called each of us to engage in ministry, spread the Gospel's message, and lead others to faith. But how can we focus on reaching the world while neglecting to do this within our own families? We cannot! Before impacting anyone else, we must ensure that our household is in order. Our primary ministry must begin within our own family. We have been entrusted with the responsibility of teaching our children in the ways of God. This encompasses praying for them, seeking God's guidance, making decisions aligned with godly principles, and maintaining a spirit of gratitude. It is our duty to instruct our children to exemplify the fruits of the Spirit, and this responsibility rests upon our shoulders.

I have seen many parents send their children to kids' ministry and youth groups and expect the church leadership to train them, but this is wrong. It's our role as parents to make sure our kids are learning from us as we continually point them to God. We must model the fruits of the Spirit and exemplify the life of Jesus in every aspect of our lives. This is such important work. Some people long for a microphone or platform yet do not want to disciple their own family. How can we ask for revival when we are not even speaking to our spouse with love? We say we want to go out and change the world but can't even do the dishes or make dinner for our own family without grumbling.

Remember, you can make the greatest impact within the walls of your own home; there is no work that is more important. We must steward well what God has given us. Love and submit to your husband. Love and disciple your children. Seek God in all that you do, and yield to the Holy Spirit. Don't forget the blessings in your own home, and never believe the lie that you need to go out to do something better or more impactful!

Scripture References

The Universal Call to Ministry
Mark 16:15

Ministry Starting at Home
1 Timothy 3:5

Parents as Primary Spiritual Educators
Deuteronomy 6:6-7

Modeling Christian Virtues
Galatians 5:22-23

Challenge

How can you disciple your children with your words and actions? Write your thoughts down below and discuss them with your spouse. Make some plans and commitments for the future together.

MAKING CHANGES

In the realm of biblical principles, if you find yourself actively involved in various ministries and your family is experiencing neglect, it is acceptable and even necessary to prioritize your family. It is crucial to step back from some or all of your responsibilities to prioritize your spouse's and children's well-being. Your primary calling is to your family before any external work or ministry.

If you are facing challenges where your children are exposed to negative influences and learning the wrong things, it is essential to take the time to reevaluate various aspects of their lives. Consider the school they attend, the sports clubs they participate in, the shows, movies, and games they're engaging with, the friends they associate with, and even certain family members. It is unacceptable if others do not respect your decisions because God has entrusted your children to your care, and you will ultimately be held responsible for their upbringing.

Focus on what is best for your family and seek God's guidance through prayer and even fasting. These are weighty decisions that will significantly impact the lives of your children. If any area of your children's lives is suffering or being negatively affected, it is crucial to step back from other commitments that divert your attention away from your children and address those issues as a priority.

Remember, putting your family first aligns with biblical principles and demonstrates your commitment to fulfilling your God-given responsibility in raising and nurturing your children.

Scripture References

Priority of Family over External Ministries
1 Timothy 5:8

Re-evaluation of Children's Influences
Proverbs 22:6

Accountability Before God
Ephesians 6:4

Seeking God's Guidance
James 1:5

The Importance of Children
Psalm 127:3

Challenge

Think about activities, habits, games, apps, and ministries you are involved in. Take a moment to write down how you think they affect your family. Share your thoughts with your wife and see if she agrees with your assessment. Make changes going forward if necessary.

FAMILY PLANNING

God's command to be fruitful and multiply does not necessarily mean that all forms of birth control are inherently wrong. The Bible also teaches us to exercise wisdom in our decisions, recognizing that there may be circumstances where additional children would present complications. However, it is essential to remember that God calls us to surrender our will to His. Even if God's plan does not involve having more children, He may prompt us to address our reluctance, as He desires our hearts to be fully surrendered to Him.

The wisest decision we can make is one that aligns with God's will. Each person's situation is unique, and God is aware of that. Seek God's guidance through fasting and prayer, both individually and together with your spouse, to discern His plan for your lives and how to move forward. In my own experience, my wife and I decided to undergo a vasectomy, believing it was the right choice. However, after some time, my wife began to sense that God was calling us to have more children, and we struggled to understand where we had gone wrong. God revealed to us that her fear of childbirth and burnout had influenced our emotional decision-making.

It is crucial to be open and sensitive to the prompting of the Holy Spirit, allowing God to guide and correct our choices. Through prayer, seeking His wisdom, and being attentive to His leadership, we can navigate these decisions in alignment with God's plan for our lives.

Scripture References

Personal Surrender to God's Will
Romans 12:2

Seeking Guidance through Fasting and Prayer
Acts 13:3 + Luke 2:37

The Role of Emotion in Decision Making
Proverbs 3:5-6 + Jeremiah 17:9

Sensitivity to the Holy Spirit
1 Corinthians 2:11-12

Challenge

Write down any birth control you are on or plan on taking, along with any procedures you have undergone. Share them with your spouse and discuss whether these methods are agreed upon moving forward. Don't be afraid to take a moment to pray together for guidance.

FOCUSING *Our* TIME

FIRST YEAR OF MARRIAGE

From a biblical perspective, the first year of marriage is a significant time of adjustment and growth as you learn to live and love as one. It's essential to be wise and intentional about how you spend your time during this period, prioritizing your relationship with your spouse above all else.

Deuteronomy 24:5 teaches us that during the first year of marriage, a man was to be free from any duties or responsibilities that could take him away from his wife. While this was a specific instruction for a different time and situation, we can still learn from the underlying principle.

As newlyweds, you should be careful not to take on too many additional responsibilities or commitments that could distract you from building a strong foundation for your marriage. Use this time to focus on learning about each other, developing good communication habits, and creating a bond that will last a lifetime.

Remember that marriage is a lifelong commitment, and the effort you invest in your relationship during the first year can set the tone for the rest of your lives together. So prioritize your marriage, seek guidance and wisdom from God, and enjoy the journey of growing together as one.

Scripture References

Love in a Marriage Relationship
Song of Solomon 8:6-7 + 1 Corinthians 13:2-7

Time for Learning and Adjustment
Deuteronomy 24:5

Seeking Divine Guidance
James 1:5

Lifelong Commitment
Matthew 19:6

Challenge

How can you prioritize your marriage though busy seasons? Write down your thoughts and discuss your ideas with your spouse.

DAY OF REST

Rest is an essential aspect of our lives, and the Bible teaches us the significance of taking time to rest and focus on God. The idea of the Sabbath has existed since the creation story in Genesis when God rested on the seventh day. In Exodus 20:8-10, God commanded us to keep the Sabbath holy and to not do any work on that day.

The Sabbath is not just about taking a day off from work or regular activities, but rather, it's a time to focus on God and deepen our relationship with Him. It's a day to worship, pray, read scripture, and spend time with our family and loved ones.

Jesus taught us that doing good deeds and helping others on the Sabbath is acceptable. Still, it's important to remember that the day's purpose is to honor God and rest in His presence.

By taking a day of rest, we can recharge ourselves physically, emotionally, and spiritually. We can also strengthen our family bond by spending quality time together and worshiping God as a family.

Scripture References

Biblical Origin of Sabbath
Genesis 2:2

Benefits of Observing the Sabbath
Matthew 11:28

Teachings of Jesus
Luke 14:5

Focus on God
Exodus 20:8-10

Purpose of the Sabbath
Mark 2:27

Challenge

Do you take a Sabbath day? If so, what does a typical Sabbath day look like to you? If not, why not? Write down your response below and take a moment to go over them with your wife.

COVERING The FAMILY

SPIRITUAL WAREFARE

In the Christian faith, we are not exempt from spiritual battles. Ephesians 6:12 reminds us that "our struggle is not against flesh and blood, but against the rulers, against the authorities, against the powers of this dark world and against the spiritual forces of evil in the heavenly realms." To face these battles, God has provided us with the Armor of God, a powerful and essential tool for our spiritual protection and victory. The first piece of armor is the Belt of Truth. Truth is foundational to our spiritual warfare. We are called to live in truth and stand firm against the lies and deceptions of the enemy. The belt of truth keeps us grounded in God's Word and enables us to discern truth from falsehood.

God has entrusted you with the important task of praying for your family, covering them in prayer, and even engaging in spiritual warfare on their behalf. While others may pray for you and your family, it is also your responsibility to pray for them diligently each day. According to the Bible, God has ordained the husband to be the head over the wife and children, and the wife to have authority over the children. This means that both parents are responsible for covering the family in prayer.

When we all unite in prayer for the well-being of our family, we align both physically and spiritually. The Bible places great emphasis on the power of agreement. Never underestimate the significance of prayer. I have witnessed how God, in His faithfulness, has answered the prayers of grandmothers that have been praying for their children and grandchildren for years, and brought salvation to entire families. He is always faithful, continuously guiding and fighting on our behalf, even before we encounter our battles.

Devote time in prayer to seek God's presence and His plans for your family. Whether in times of ease or difficulty, seek Him wholeheartedly. When the enemy comes with his deceptive tactics, respond with spiritual wareafare. Let us put on the full armor of God, turn directly to God and lay the situation before the Lord. God will answer with His mighty power and authority.

Scripture References

Role of Parents in Spiritual Warfare
Ephesians 6:12

The Comprehensive Armor of God
Ephesians 6:14-18

Hierarchy of Spiritual Responsibility
Ephesians 5:23 + Proverbs 31:26-28

Power of Communal Intercession
1 Timothy 2:1-2

God's Faithfulness and Power
Psalm 145:18

Challenge

Think about a time that you can devote to God. Make a plan below for when you can commit to praying with God about the plans He has given you for your family.

PRAY TOGETHER

The power of unity should never be underestimated. As the Scriptures remind us, a person standing alone can be attacked and defeated, but two can stand back-to-back and conquer. Three are even better, for a triple-braided cord is not easily broken. When God is at the center of your marriage, it can not be easily broken!

It is vital to make a conscious effort to pray together with your spouse. Through joint prayer, you will grow closer to one another in a physical and spiritual sense and establish a solid foundation for your marriage. This foundation is built upon God and His divine plans and purposes for your lives together.

If you have not already met with your spouse to communicate and discuss matters within your home, set aside dedicated time for this purpose, and include a prayer time. Praying together for every situation and challenge you encounter will invite God's presence into your marriage.

If you feel apprehensive about praying together, let go of any worries. It is not about putting on a show or offering the most eloquent prayer. Simply approach God in the same way you communicate with your spouse. Share your heart honestly and sincerely, for God hears and answers prayers because He is faithful.

There is a saying: "A family that prays together stays together." Speaking from experience, this greatly benefited my family as we started praying together. It is so wonderful to experience God's grace and mercy in our prayer life.

Scripture References

Unity in Marriage Through Prayer
Ecclesiastes 4:12

Importance of Praying with Spouse
1 Thessalonians 5:17 + James 5:16

The Simplicity of Prayer
Matthew 6:7

Challenge

Write down some topics you'd like your husband to pray about. Make some time to pray with your husband, taking turns to read each other's topics and praying for them out loud together.

A New BEGINNING

AS A GODLY HUSBAND

HUSBAND AFTER GOD

It's been a pleasure to share our marriage devotional with you, and we're grateful you took the time to engage with it. Our hope is that it's been a valuable tool in strengthening your role as a godly husband and deepening your connection with your wife. Our intention with this book was to offer insights from a biblical perspective on various topics that, in today's society, are often misunderstood or misrepresented. We understand that the journey of marriage can be full of challenges, and the subjects we've explored may have been thought-provoking for you. They certainly were for us during our research and study phase. Our aim is that the scriptures and biblical principles within these pages have been a source of strength and empowerment for you.

At GFW, our motto is, "When God has our hearts, everything else falls into place." This, we believe, is the foundation of a fulfilling life. God's faithfulness in providing for us is unwavering. Stay close to Him, and watch as He works wonders in your life.

If you've found encouragement and support in this book, we'd be honored if you'd share it with others. Many people struggle in silence, and there's a real need for the kind of support and guidance this book offers. In these challenging times, when family structures are often under threat, it's crucial for the church to confront falsehoods and stand firm in the truth of God's Word, praying for and supporting each other.

Lastly, if you've journeyed through this book solo, we'd like to let you know that there's a companion devotional designed for your wife or fiancée. It's available for order on our website, gfwlife.com, and we think it could be a great resource for her as well.

Challenge

This book has provided you with many insightful lessons on being a godly husband. Now, it's time to put these learnings into practice by writing a heartfelt love letter to your wife. Start by seeking guidance through prayer, asking God to help you find the perfect words to express your feelings. Your letter can take any form you feel drawn to – be it a message of affirmation, a heartfelt confession, a poem, a song, or a blend of these elements. Once you've finished writing, pray over your letter, seeking God's wisdom on the best way to share it with your wife. Enjoy this creative process and remain attentive to God's guidance at every step.

Prayer for Your Marraige

Dear Lord, thank you for bringing this reader to the truths within Your Word. Thank you for the training and equipping they have received, and I ask that You help them to remember Your truths. Lord, I pray for perfect harmony within their marriage.

I declare and decree that every evil spirit of confusion, discord, discontentment, disharmony, bitterness, anger, adultery, and unforgiveness have no place within their marriage. I declare this in the name of Jesus Christ. I also ask God that You would anoint their home and bring Your Peace and Your Spirit to dwell in their house.

I decree now that satan will not kill, steal, or destroy your marriage and that no weapon formed against this union shall prosper. I come against every plot of the enemy to use ungodly sources to speak against, strategize, or form evil schemes against your marriage. I thank You, God, that what You have placed together no man can separate. I ask that You would seal this prayer upon this reader's marriage, in Jesus name. Amen!

Printed in the USA
CPSIA information can be obtained
at www.ICGtesting.com
LVHW071208020624
782037LV00036B/994

9 798869 059932